Place value, ordering and rounding

PV1.1 Introducing thousands

TB pages 5–6

A1 a 2000 b 400
    c 60   d 200

A2 two thousand eight hundred and thirty
    three thousand four hundred
    one thousand four hundred and sixty
    seven thousand two hundred and fifty-four
    five thousand seven hundred and ninety-six

A3 a 6437 = **6000** + 400 + 30 + 7
    b 2185 = 2000 + **100** + 80 + 5
    c 9279 = 9000 + 200 + **70** + 9
    d 3513 = **3000** + 500 + 10 + **3**

B1 a 2468, 2486, 2648, 2684, 2846, 2864,
       4268, 4286, 4628, 4682, 4826, 4862,
       6248, 6284, 6428, 6482, 6824, 6842,
       8246, 8264, 8426, 8462, 8624, 8642
    b 2468, 2486, 6428, 6482, 8426, 8462
    c 6284, 6482

C1 Children's biggest and smallest 5-digit numbers, e.g. 76 310 and 10 367

PV1.2 Changing thousands

TB page 7

A1 a 927   b 716   c 1600
    d 1059 e 2026   f 8070
    g 1150 h 3755   i 6413

A2

altitude	+ 1	+ 10	+ 100	+ 1000
146	147	157	257	1257
839	840	850	950	1950
3025	3026	3036	3136	4136
4966	4967	4977	5077	6077
7890	7891	7901	8001	9001

A3 Children's check, e.g. subtract 1111 from each final number

B1 CM 1

B2 Children's own 4 loops using 4-digit numbers

CM 1

1
4126 → 4226 → 5226 → 5216 → 4216 → 4116
7019 → 6019 → 5919 → 5909 → 6909 → 6919 → 7019
3990 → 4990 → 5000 → 4900 → 3900 → 4000 → 3990
8000 → 7990 → 8000 → 9000 → 9100 → 8100 → 8000

2 a The start and finish numbers are the same.
   b This happens because we add on and take away the same numbers.

CM 2

1 549 → 559 → 659
   57 → 67 → 167
   186 → 196 → 296
   404 → 414 → 514
   1 → 11 → 111

2 666 → 1666 → 1656
   810 → 1810 → 1800
   1287 → 2287 → 2277
   6042 → 7042 → 7032

3 Children's own number trails

PV1.3 Comparing numbers and measurements

TB pages 8–9

A1 a

fuel	90 l
height	5000 m
speed	270 km/h

b

fuel	50 l
height	4500 m
speed	420 km/h

B1 a Red Alert because 50 < 90
    b 40 l because 90 − 50 = 40
    c Blue Baron because 5000 > 4500
    d 500 m because 5000 − 4500 = 500
    e 150 km/h because 420 − 270 = 150

C1 Children's own inequality sentences

PV2.1 Ordering 4-digit numbers

TB page 10

A1 **4395**, 4396, 4397, 4398, **4399**, **4400**

A2 1782, 1827, 2178, 2187, 2781

A3 a 5 of: 2002, 2004, ... 2096, 2098
    b 5 of: 5401, 5403, ... 5497, 5499
    c any 5 numbers in the range 7600–7699
    d any 5 numbers in the range 4501–4509

C1 True. There are 10 palindromic 4-digit numbers that start and end in 1:
    1001, 1111, 1221, 1331, 1441, 1551, 1661, 1771, 1881, 1991
    Similarly there are 10 that start and end in 2, 3, 4, 5, 6, 7, 8 and 9.

PV2.2 Multiplying by 10

TB page 11

A1 a 36 × 10 = 360
    b 53 × 10 = 530
    c 420 × 10 = 4200

A2 a 15 × 10 = **150**
       39 × 10 = **390**
       84 × 10 = **840**
    b 9 × 10 = **90**
       18 × 10 = **180**
       27 × 10 = **270**
    c 170 × 10 = **1700**
       260 × 10 = **2600**
       120 × 10 = **1200**

B1 a 5 × 10 = **50**
       50 × 10 = **500**
       500 × 10 = **5000**
    b 37 × 10 = **370**
       370 × 10 = **3700**
       3700 × 10 = **37 000**
    c 64 × 10 = **640**
       640 × 10 = **6400**
       6400 × 10 = **64 000**
    d Children's own × 10 and × 100 patterns

B2 a 257, 275, 527, 572, 725, 752
    b 2570, 2750, 5270, 5720, 7250, 7520
    c Same order as above.

PV2.3 Dividing by 10

TB pages 12–13

A1 a 90 daffodils make **9** bunches.
       60 daffodils in 6 bunches.
    b **100** roses make 10 bunches.
       110 roses in **11** bunches.
    c 500 petunias make **50** trays.
       700 petunias in 70 trays.
    d 300 crocus make **3** boxes.
       1000 crocus in 10 boxes.

A2 a Children's dividing-by-10 machine and 7 numbers tested in it

B1 a 1 flower pot costs   £3
       10 flower pots cost   £30
       100 flower pots cost   £300
       5000 flower pots cost   £15 000
    b 1 house plant costs   £12
       10 house plants cost   £120
       100 house plants cost   £1200
       1000 house plants cost   £12 000
    c 100 m of fencing costs   £2000
       10 m of fencing costs   £200
       1 m of fencing costs   £20
    d 100 kg of gravel costs   £170
       10 kg of gravel costs   £17
       1 kg of gravel costs   £1.70

B2 40 → **4**, 70 → **7**, 100 → **10**, 900 → **90**,
    500 → 50, 8000 → **800**, 9000 → **900**

C1 For example:
    a 1 → 100 → 10, 2 → 200 → 20, ...
    b 20 → 2000 → 200
       25 → 2500 → 250
       39 → 3900 → 390

PV2.4 Matching examples

TB pages 14–15

A1 a 7 cm × 10 = 70 cm
       12 cm × 10 = **120 cm**
       25 cm × 10 = **250 cm**
    b 70 cm × 10 = **700 cm**
       120 cm × 10 = **1200 cm**
       250 cm × 10 = **2500 cm**
    c 7 cm × 100 = **700 cm**
       12 cm × 100 = **1200 cm**
       25 cm × 100 = **2500 cm**

A2 a   4p × 10 = **40p**
        10p × 10 = **100p**
        80p × 10 = **800p** or **£8**

    b   40p × 10 = **400p**
        100p × 10 = **1000p** or **£10**
        £8 × 10 = **£80**

    c   4p × 100 = **400p** or **£4**
        10p × 100 = **1000p** or **£10**
        80p × 100 = **8000p** or **£80**

B1 a   6 × 100 = **600** pens
        60 × 10 = **600** pens

    b   **15** × 100 = 1500 jotters
        150 × 10 = 1500 jotters

    c   **36** × 100 = 3600 glue sticks
        360 × 10 = 3600 glue sticks

B2 a   24 × 10 × 10 = 2400 pencils
    b   £300
    c   10 stars cost 20p, 1 star costs 2p.

C1 For example:
    There are 10 crayons in a pack and 200 packs in a box. How many in 1 box?
    There are 100 cubes in a bag and 50 bags in a box. How many cubes in 1 box?
    31 elastic bands in a pack, 100 packs in a box. How many elastic bands in 1 box?
    You get 50 pegs in a pack, 10 packs in a bag, and 15 bags in a box. How many pegs in 1 box?

CM 6

1   Race A: 50, 200, 100, 700, 80, 900.
            500, 2000, 1000, 7000, 800, 9000.
    Race B: 670, 4000, 530, 9000, 820, 7000.
            6700, 40 000, 5300, 90 000, 8200, 70 000.

2   The finish numbers for hare and tortoise are the same.

PV3.1 Using negative numbers

TB pages 16–17

B1 a   step 2   b   step 4
    c   step −3   d   step −5

B2

+2	down 2	step 0
−1	up 3	step 2
+4	down 6	step −2
−3	up 3	step 0
+5	down 10	step −5
−6	up 5	step −1

C1 For example:
    −6 + 6 = 0
    −5 + 6 = 1
    ...
    −1 + 6 = 5

C2 For example:
    5 − 3 = 2
    4 − 3 = 1
    ...
    −3 − 3 = −6

CM 7

1   Check that thermometers are coloured to the correct levels.
2   b and d show temperatures above 0°C
    a, c, e and f show temperatures below 0°C
3   The warmest temperature is d and the coldest is e.

PV3.2 Ordering on a number line

TB pages 18–19

A1 a   0   b   2   c   4
    d   −3   e   −6   f   −8

A2 a   any 2 of −1, 0, 1, 2
    b   any 2 of 1, 2, 3, 4
    c   any 2 of −3, −2, −1, 0
    d   any 2 of −11, −10, −9

B2 a   −12°C, −9°C, −4°C, −2°C, 0°C, 6°C, 18°C, 23°C

B3 a   Calgary
    b   Delhi
    c   London, Athens, Delhi
    d   Calgary, Moscow, Toronto, Brussels

C1 a   Paris   b   Moscow
    c   London   d   Delhi

C2 Children's own temperature problems

PV3.3 Reading scales

TB page 20

- B1
  - a 7 m
  - b 14 m
  - c 60 m
  - d 0.6 m
  - e 275 m
  - f 508 m
- B2
  - a 20 ml
  - b 75 ml
  - c 350 ml
  - d 170 ml
- B3
  - a 35 kg
  - b 2.5 kg
  - c 240 g
- B4
  - a −3°C
  - b −6°C
  - c 0°C and −3°C

CM 9

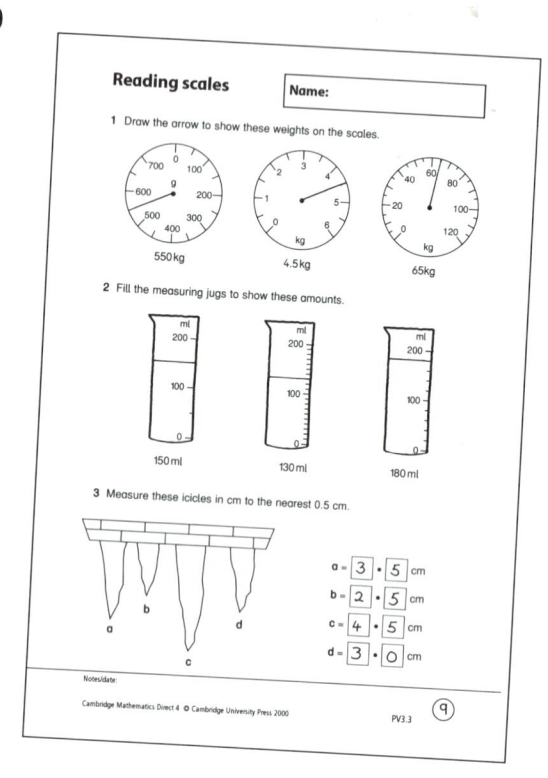

PV4.1 Collections and numbers

TB pages 21–22

- A1
  - a about 90 bubbles
  - b For example: There are 9 strings of bubbles and each has about 10 bubbles.
- A2 Look for reasonable estimates, for example:
  - a 220 spots
  - b There are 11 groups of spots and each has about 20 spots.
- A3 Children's estimating puzzles
- B1
  - a about 80
  - b about 40
  - c The middle box has about twice as many as the box on the left.
    The box on the left has about half as many as the middle box.
    The middle box has about 4 times as many as the box on the right.
    The box on the right has about quarter as many as the middle box.
    The box on the left has about twice as many as the box on the right.
    The box on the right has about half as many as the box on the left.
- B2 Children's 3 boxes of shells and comparing sentences
- C1
  - a There may be enough shells.
  - b About 220 children could have one.
- C2
  - a About 4 small tins
  - b About 2 big tins (with some left over)

PV4.2 Using number lines to round

TB page 23

- A1
  - a 670
  - b 860
  - c 310
  - d 490
  - e 550
  - f 610
- A2
  - a 300
  - b 810
  - c 700
  - d 690
  - e 700
  - f 390
- A3
  - a 231 rounds to 230. The other numbers round to 240.
  - b 656 rounds to 660. The other numbers round to 650.
  - c 701 rounds to 700. The other numbers round to 710.
- C1 For example:
  - a 270
  - b 265, 266, 267, 268, 269, 270, 271, 272, 273, 274
  - c 9
- C2 For example:
  There are always 10 numbers that round, to the nearest 10, to a multiple of 10. The difference between the largest and the smallest is always 9.
  This is because the largest is 4 more than the number and the smallest is 5 less than the number.

CM 11

1. 423
2. 667
3. 390
4. 551
5. 860
6. 720

CM 12

1. Most round to 350.
   The odd one out is 356.
2. Most round to 710.
   The odd one out is 702.
3. Most round to 650.
   The odd one out is 642.
4. 290: 288 and 294
   350: 345 and 351
   670: 671 and 672
   840: 835, 838 and 843
5. a 295, 296, 297, 298, 299, 300, 301, 302, 303, 304
   b 595, 596, 597, 598, 599, 600, 601, 602, 603, 604

PV4.3 Rounding to 10, 100

TB page 24

B1 a 245, 246, 247, 248, 249, 250, 251, 252, 253, 254
    b To the nearest 100:
       245, 246, 247, 248, 249 round to 200
       250, 251, 252, 253, 254 round to 300
    c The numbers round to 2 different 100s

B2 a 445, 446, 447, 448, 449, 450, 451, 452, 453, 454
    b To the nearest 100:
       445, 446, 447, 448, 449 round to 400
       450, 451, 452, 453, 454 round to 500
    a 745, 746, 747, 748, 749, 750, 751, 752, 753, 754
    b To the nearest 100:
       745, 746, 747, 748, 749 round to 700
       750, 751, 752, 753, 754 round to 800
    c The numbers round to 2 different 100s

B3 20 numbers in the range 450–549

C1 a 350   b 449   c 99

C2 a The smallest number will be 50 less than the chosen multiple.
    b The largest number will be 49 more than the chosen multiple.
    c The difference will be 99.

C3 999

PV4.4 Approximating

TB pages 25–26

A1 a about 340 + 80 = 420
    b about 660 + 230 = 890
    c about 300 + 700 = 1000
    d about 480 + 400 = 880

A2 d is the best

B1 a about 80 + 130 = 210
    b about 100 + 110 = 210
    c about 100 + 140 = 240
    d about 110 + 160 = 270
    e about 150 + 210 = 360

B2 a 213   b 211

B3 The estimate for Monday was 3 less than the actual number and for Friday it was 1 more than the actual number.

C1 a (any number 795–804) + (any number 495–504)
    b (any number 550–649) + (any number 250–349)
    c (any number 4150–4249) + (any number 3650–3749)

C2 Children's problems about the small fish tanks

CM 13

1 A 70   B 160   C 50
2 A + B = 70 + 160 = 230
   B + C = 160 + 50 = 210
   C + A = 50 + 70 = 120
   A + B + C = 70 + 160 + 50 = 280

Properties of numbers and number sequences

N1.1   1s, 10s, 100s and 1000s

TB pages 27–28

A1 a 507, 137, 213, 484
    b 493, 123, 199, 470
    c 570, 200, 276, 547
    d 430, 60, 136, 407

A2 a 500, 510, 520, **530, 540, 550**
    b 650, 750, 850, **950, 1050, 1150**
    c 2240, 2340, 2440, **2540, 2640, 2740**

B1 Children's sequences of 5 numbers. The starting numbers 5300 and 7060 avoid negative numbers when counting back in 1000s.

C1 a 416 + 500 [**916**] + **1000** [1916]
    b 380 + 600 [**980**] + **2000** [2980]
    c 725 + 700 [**1425**] + **4000** [5425]

C2 Children's own adding puzzles

CM 14

1 478, 479, 480, 481, 482, 483, 484
2 478, 488, 498, 508, 518, 528, 538
3 478, 578, 678, 778, 878, 978, 1078
4 478, 1478, 2478, 3478, 4478, 5478, 6478

N1.2   Odds and evens 1

TB page 29

A1 a odd: 29, 105, 447, 863
       even: 6, 54, 78, 310
    b The last digit of an odd number is **1** or **3** or **5** or **7** or **9**.

B1 a Totals of children's 6 chosen pairs; there are 21 possible pairs.
    b When we add 2 odd numbers the answer is **even**.

B2 a 6 of:
       23 − 21 = 2
       23 − 19 = 4   23 − 17 = 6
       23 − 15 = 8   23 − 11 = 12
       21 − 19 = 2   21 − 17 = 4
       21 − 15 = 6   21 − 11 = 10
       19 − 17 = 2   19 − 15 = 4
       19 − 11 = 8   17 − 15 = 2
       17 − 11 = 4   15 − 11 = 4

   b The difference between a pair of odd numbers is **even**.

C1 CM 15 question 2

CM 15

1 a

+	1	2	3	4	5	6
1	**2**	3	**4**	5	**6**	7
2	3	**4**	5	**6**	7	**8**
3	**4**	5	**6**	7	**8**	9
4	5	**6**	7	**8**	9	**10**
5	**6**	7	**8**	9	**10**	11
6	7	**8**	9	**10**	11	**12**

   b Even numbers are **bold** in the table.
   c Number of even totals 18
      Number of odd totals   18

2 You would expect results to tend towards the average of:
   a score 2, 1; score 3, 2; score 4, 3; score 5, 4; score 6, 5; score 7, 6; score 8, 5; score 9, 4; score 10, 3; score 11, 2; score 12, 1.
   b Number of even scores 18
      Number of odd scores   18

N1.3   Odds and evens 2

TB pages 30–31

A1 CM 16

B1 a 5 + 5 + 5 = 15
       7 + 7 + 7 = 21
       13 + 13 + 13 = 39
    b 9 + 9 + 9 = 27
       11 + 11 + 11 = 33
       15 + 15 + 15 = 45

B2 a e.g. 5 + 5 + 9 or 6 + 6 + 7 = 19
       e.g. 20 + 20 + 7 or 15 + 15 + 17 = 47
       e.g. 30 + 30 + 5 or 5 + 25 + 35 = 65
    b Either all the numbers are odd, or 2 are even and 1 odd.
    c Children's trio totals

C1 a 45 = 2 × 22 + 1
       51 = 2 × 25 + 1
       69 = 2 × 34 + 1
       87 = 2 × 43 + 1
       93 = 2 × 46 + 1
    b Children's test of 6 more odd numbers

CM 16

15 = 3 + 11 + 1 or 3 + 9 + 3 or 3 + 7 + 5
27 = 7 + 19 + 1 or 7 + 17 + 3 or 7 + 15 + 5
   or 7 + 13 + 7 or 7 + 11 + 9
35 = 19 + 15 + 1 or 19 + 13 + 3
   or 19 + 11 + 5 or 19 + 9 + 7
23 = 11 + 11 + 1 or 11 + 9 + 3 or 11 + 7 + 5
41 = 7 + 33 + 1 or 7 + 31 + 3 or ...
   or 7 + 17 + 17
39 = 13 + 25 + 1 or 13 + 23 + 3 or ...
   or 13 + 13 + 13

Children's own choices of numbers

N1.4 Fours

TB page 32

A1 a 0, 2, 4, 6, 8, 10, 12, 14, 16, 18, 20
    b 0, 4, 8, 12, 16, 20
    c 40, 38, 36, 34, 32, 30, 28, 26, 24, 22, 20
    d 40, 36, 32, 28, 24, 20

B1 a They are **multiples** of 4 and are **divisible** by 4.
    b 20 → 10 → 5
       22 → 11 → x
       25 → x
       28 → 14 → 7
       32 → 16 → 8
       37 → x
       20, 28 and 32 are divisible by 4.

B2 Divisible by 4 test: A number has to be an **even** number; divide exactly by 2 and divide exactly by **2** again.

CM 17

Grid 1: Alternate numbers in the 2, 4 and 6 columns are shaded, starting with 4, 8 and 12. 42 and 46 will not be in the sequence.
Grid 2: Numbers are shaded diagonally, sloping down from 4.
Grid 3: The 4 and 8 columns are shaded.

Grid 2 is the only one where the shading is not in columns.

CM 18

1 White Light run: 8, 12, 16, 28, 32, 48, 56, 64, 100
   Black Forest run: 5, 18, 26, 29, 34, 42, 46, 50, 54

2 Children's own sets of 'multiples' and 'not multiples'.

N1.5 Threes

TB pages 33–34

A1 CM 19.

A2 a 2 + 4 = 6, so 24 is divisible by 3.
    b 2 + 9 = 11, so 29 is not divisible by 3.
    c 3 + 6 = 9, so 36 is divisible by 3.
    d 4 + 1 = 5, so 41 is not divisible by 3.
    e 4 + 5 = 9, so 45 is divisible by 3.

B1

	divisible by 3	not divisible by 3
odd	15, 21, 27, 39	19, 23, 31, 35
even	12, 24, 42	14, 38, 40, 46

B2 Add the digits to see whether their sum is a 3, 6 or 9, and find out whether 102 is a multiple of 3. For example:
1 + 0 + 2 = 3
3 × 30 = 90, 3 × 4 = 12 so
3 × 34 = 102, and 102 is a multiple of 3.

C1 10 of:
345, 354, 435, 453, 534, 543
357, 375, 537, 573, 735, 753
405, 450, 504, 540
507, 570, 705, 750

C2 4-digit numbers divisible by 3:
3045, 3054, 3405, 3450, 3504, 3540
4035, 4053, 4305, 4350, 4503, 4530
5034, 5043, 5304, 5340, 5403, 5430
3057, 3075, 3507, 3570, 3705, 3750
5037, 5073, 5307, 5370, 5703, 5730
7035, 7053, 7305, 7350, 7503, 7530

Check that the trick works by adding the digits and if they total 3, 6 or 9, check that the number is divisible by 3, using a different method.

CM 19

1 Grid 1: Numbers are shaded on diagonals from 3, 6 and 21.
   Grid 2: Numbers are shaded in 2 columns from 3 and 6.

2 With a 10 × 10 grid the shading patterns is diagonal, going down and left.

N2.1 2-, 3-, 4- and 5-steps

TB pages 35–36

A1 a 13, 23, 33, 43, **53, 63, 73, 83**
       The pattern goes up in 10s.
       The units digit does not change; the tens digit goes up 1 each time.
   b 32, 37, 42, 47, **52, 57, 62, 67**
       The pattern goes up in 5s. The units digit alternates between 2 and 7; the tens digit goes up 1 every second time.
   c 107, 105, 103, 101, **99, 97, 95, 93**
       The pattern goes down in 2s. The units digit is always odd and in the pattern 7, 5, 3, 1, 9, 7, …
   d 87, 91, 95, 99, **103, 107, 111, 115**
       The pattern goes up in 4s. The units digit is always odd and in the pattern 7, 1, 5, 9, 3, 7, …

A2 a 103   b 77   c 89   d 123

B1 a 3652, 3552, 3452, 3352, **3252, 3152, 3052**
       The pattern goes down in 100s. Only the hundreds digit changes (until you cross the thousands boundary).
   b 218, 213, 208, 203, **198, 193, 188**
       The pattern goes down in 5s. The units digit alternates between 8 and 3.
   c 54, 57, 60, 63, **66, 69, 72**
       The pattern goes up in 3s.
       The units digit is in the pattern 4, 7, 0, 3, 6, 9, 2, 5, 8, 1, 4, …

B2 a 2752   b 173   c 81

B3 The 10th number is 84.
    The 20th number is 114.
    The 30th number is 144.
    The 100th number is 354.

C1 a The rule is add 4, starting from 31.
       The units digit is in the pattern 1, 5, 9, 3, 7, 1, …
       The units digits are in a circle pattern of odd digits.
    b The rule is subtract 4, starting from 52.
       The units digit is in the pattern 2, 8, 4, 0, 6, 2, …
       The units digits are in a circle pattern of even digits.

C2 With steps of 2 the units digits are in a circle pattern of even numbers if the starting number is even, and of odd numbers if the starting number is odd.
    With steps of 3 the units digits are in a circle pattern that includes all digits.
    With steps of 5 the units digits alternate between 2 numbers with a difference of 5.
    With steps of 10 the units digits are all the same. The 10s digit changes by 1 each time.
    With steps of 100 the units and tens digits are all the same. The 100s digit changes by 1 each time.

N2.3 Multiples

TB page 37

B1 a In the 1st grid the 3 and 6 columns are shaded.
       In the 2nd grid the shaded numbers slope down to the left from 3 and 12.
    b In both patterns every 3rd number is shaded.
    c One is a column pattern, the other is a diagonal pattern.

B2 Children's choice of grids to show pattern of 5s

C1 Investigation of different grids and multiples

CM 40 (Support)

Children should find that the 2, 4, 6, 8 and 10 columns are marked, and that every multiple of 4 is also a multiple of 2, but that every 2nd multiple of 2 is not a multiple of 4.
Similarly they should find that the 5 and 10 columns are marked, and that all multiples of 10 are also multiples of 5, but the odd multiples of 5 are not multiples of 10.
With multiples of 3 children will find a diagonal pattern, with diagonals sloping down to the left from 3, 6, and 9.

CM 20

1 On the 1st grid the pattern slopes down to the right, on the 2nd grid the pattern slopes down to the left.
2 On both grids the pattern slopes down diagonally to the left.
   On the 1st grid there are 2 parallel diagonal lines, but on the 2nd there is only 1.

N2.4 More multiples

TB pages 38–39

B1 Children's number snake. Multiples of 25 will be ringed in red, multiples of 50 in red and yellow, multiples of 100 in red, yellow and blue.

B2 a Halfway between 2 multiples of 50 is a multiple of **25**.
   b Halfway between 2 multiples of **100** is a multiple of 50.
   c Every 5th multiple of 5 is a multiple of **25**.
   d Every 4th multiple of 25 is a multiple of 100.
   e Every 2nd multiple of 25 is a multiple of **50**.
   f 150 and 200 are both multiples of 50. Halfway between them is **175** which is a multiple of **25**.

C1 a Hari 20 days, Winston 4 days, Emma 2 days, Shanazara 1 day.
   b Hari 100 days, Winston 20 days, Emma 10 days, Shanazara 5 days.
   c Hari 200 days, Winston 40 days, Emma 20 days, Shanazara 10 days.
   d Hari 2000 days, Winston 400 days, Emma 200 days, Shanazara 100 days.

C2 a two 50p coins
   b five 5p coins
   c Winston takes 32 days to save £8.
      25p × 4 × 8 = £8

C3 Investigation of 75

N3.1 Extending counting patterns

TB page 40

All the numbers in the 8-step sequence are also in the 4-step and 2-step sequences.
All the numbers in the 4-step sequence are also in the 2-step sequence.
Every 2nd number in the 4-step sequence is in the 8-step sequence.
Every 2nd number in the 2-step sequence is in the 4-step sequence.
Every 4th number in the 2-step sequence is in the 8-step sequence.

CM 21

1 6, 4, 2, 0, −2, −4, −6, −8, −10
2 9, 5, 1, −3, −7
3 −8, −5, −2, 1, 4, 7, 10, 13
4 −10, −5, 0, 5, 10, 15, 20, 25
5 10, 5, 0, −5, −10
6 10, 7, 4, 1, −2, −5, −8
7 5, 3, 1, −1, −3, −5, −7, −9, −11, −13
8 7, 2, −3, −8, −13, −18, −23
9 11, 7, 3, −1, −5, −9, −13, −17
10 5, 2, −1, −4, −7, −10, −13, −16

N3.2 Matching examples

TB pages 41–42

B1 a 24, 32, 48, 56, 64, 76, 80
   b 21, 24, 42, 48, 51, 63, 69, 93

B2 a For example: Multiples of 4 are even. The units digit is 0, 4 or 8 when the tens digit is even. The units digit is 2 or 6 when the tens digit is odd.
   b For example: 36, 96, 12, 44, 28, 40
   c For example: The digits of multiples of 3 add up to 3, 6 or 9.
   d For example: 12 (1 + 2 = 3),
      36 (3 + 6 = 9),
      96 (9 + 6 = 15, 1 + 5 = 6)

B3 Children's investigation of multiples of their chosen number

C1 a Every other multiple of 4 is also a multiple of 8.
   b Multiples of 4 are 4, <u>8</u>, 12, <u>16</u>, 20, <u>24</u>, 28, <u>32</u>, ...
      Multiples of 8 are underlined.

C2 a Every 4th multiple of 3 is also a multiple of 12.
   b Multiples of 4 are 3, 6, 9, <u>12</u>, 15, 18, 21, <u>24</u>, 27, 30, ...
      Multiples of 12 are underlined.

C3 a Every 3rd multiple of 5 is also a multiple of 15.
   b Multiples of 5 are 5, 10, <u>15</u>, 20, 25, <u>30</u>, ...
      Multiples of 15 are underlined.

CM 22

1. 4, 34, 18, 12, 30, 42, 38, 16, 6, 10 ringed.
   All even numbers are multiples of 2.
2. For example: 4, 8, 12, 16, 20, 24, ...
   For example: All multiples of 4 are even numbers that can be divided by 2 then divided by 2 again.
3. All multiples of 5 end in 5 or 0 (have units digit 5 or 0). For example: 5, 10, 15, 20, ...

N3.3 Patterns and puzzles

TB page 43

B1 For example:
   $1 = 3 - 2$
   $2 = 4 - 2$
   $3 = 2 + 1$
   $4 = 3 + 1$
   $5 = 4 + 1$
   $6 = 3 \times 2$
   $7 = 4 + 3$
   $8 = 4 \times 2$
   $9 = 4 + 3 + 2$
   $10 = (4 + 1) \times 2$
   $11 = 4 \times 3 - 1$
   $12 = 4 \times 3$
   $13 = 4 \times 3 + 1$
   $14 = 4 \times 3 + 2$
   $15 = (4 + 1) \times 3$
   $16 = (3 + 1) \times 4$
   $17 = (4 + 2) \times 3 - 1$
   $18 = (4 + 2) \times 3$
   $19 = (4 + 2) \times 3 + 1$
   $20 = (3 + 2) \times 4$

B2 a Children's numbers from those in b
    b 21, 24, 27, 30, 33, 36, 39, 42, 45, 48
       They are all multiples of / divisible by 3.

C1 a $7 \times 9 = 63$ $8 \times 8 = 64$
    b $10 \times 12 = 120$ $11 \times 11 = 121$
    c For example
       $5 \times 7 = 35$ $6 \times 6 = 36$
       The product of the inside number multiplied by itself is 1 greater than the product of the outside numbers.
    d With 4 consecutive numbers, the product of the outside numbers is 2 less than the product of the inside numbers.

C2 a 10 and 11; 6 and 7; 8 and 9; 14 and 15.
    b Children's own consecutive number puzzles

CM 23

1. The house numbers are:
   6, 8, 10, 12, 14, 16, 18, 20, 22, 24
   7, 9, 11, 13, 15, 17, 19, 21, 23, 25
2. 14, **18**, 22, **26**, 30, **34**, 38, **42**, 46
   The numbers increase by 4, starting at 14.
3. **16**, 20, **24**, 28, 32, **36**, 40, 44, **48**
   The numbers are multiples of 4 starting at 16.
4. The difference between the numbers on consecutive houses on each side of the street is 2.
5. Children's own puzzles

N3.4 Grid puzzles

TB page 44

C1

3	16	9	22	15
20	8	21	14	2
7	25	13	1	19
24	12	5	18	6
11	4	17	10	23

C2 For example:

```
      1
    6   7
  8       3
5   2   4   9
```

C3 For example:

6	7	2
1	5	9
8	3	4

1	15	14	4
12	6	7	9
8	10	11	5
13	3	2	16

CM 24

1.

9	0	6
2	5	8
4	10	1

Magic number 15

2.

7	8	3
2	6	10
9	4	5

Magic number 18

3
```
      6
    5   2
  1   7   4    Magic number 12
```
4
```
      3
    10  9
  4   8   5    Magic number 17
```
5

16	2	3	13
5	11	10	8
9	7	6	12
4	14	15	1

Magic number 34

6, 7 For example:
```
      5              3
    3   4          5   6
  2   7   1      2   7   1
```

N3.5 Growing patterns

TB pages 45–46

B1, B2a

Square	1	2	3	4	5	6	7
Dots on perimeter	4	8	12	16	20	24	28
Dots inside	0	1	4	9	16	25	36

B2b The number of dots on the perimeter are the multiples of 4.
The number of dots inside are the square numbers starting with 0.

C1

Size of pond in squares	Number of slabs round pond
1	8
4	12
9	16
16	20
25	24
36	28

C2 a The size of pond is the pattern of square numbers.
   b The number of slabs round the side are multiples of 4 starting with 8.
   c The number of slabs round the outside is 4 times the number of slabs on 1 side, plus 4.

Fractions and decimals

F1.1 Fractions of shapes

TB page 47

B1   a $\frac{3}{8}$ b $\frac{3}{5}$ c $\frac{1}{6}$
      d $\frac{5}{10}$ or $\frac{1}{2}$ e $\frac{1}{4}$ f $\frac{2}{5}$

B2   CM 26

C1   Children's labels showing equivalence of $\frac{3}{4}$ and $\frac{6}{8}$; $\frac{1}{2}$, $\frac{3}{6}$ and $\frac{5}{10}$; $\frac{3}{5}$ and ...

CM 25

1. Check that children have shaded the correct number of sections.
2. There are 9 sections in the triangle. $\frac{4}{9} + \frac{5}{9} = 1$

CM 26

1. Circle divided into $\frac{1}{8}$s, 4 parts shaded.
2. Hexagon divided into $\frac{1}{6}$s, 4 parts shaded.
3. Rectangle divided into $\frac{1}{10}$s, 5 parts shaded.
4. Rectangle divided into $\frac{1}{10}$s, 8 parts shaded.
5. Rectangle divided into $\frac{1}{5}$s, 3 parts shaded.
6. Circle divided into $\frac{1}{8}$s, 6 parts shaded.
7. Rectangle divided into $\frac{1}{5}$s, 2 parts shaded.
8. Hexagon divided into $\frac{1}{3}$s, 1 part shaded.
9. Rectangle divided into $\frac{1}{5}$s, 1 part shaded.
10. $\frac{4}{8}$ and $\frac{5}{10}$ are equal to $\frac{1}{2}$.
11. $\frac{4}{6} + \frac{1}{3} = 1$ $\frac{3}{5} + \frac{2}{5} = 1$ $\frac{8}{10} + \frac{1}{5} = 1$

CM 27

Check that children have coloured the right number of sections and written the correct fraction in each box.

F1.2 Fractions of numbers 1

TB pages 48–49

A1   a $\frac{2}{5}$ b $\frac{1}{8}$
      c $\frac{2}{3}$ d $\frac{5}{6}$

A2   a   6   b   10
      c   14   d   25
      e   100

A3   4 worms, 5 beetles, 8 spiders, 10 snails, 50 ants

B1   a   11   b   9
      c   44 ÷ 4 = 11

B2   a   14   b   7

B3   a   16   b   8

C1   27

C2   a   For example:
      $\frac{3}{4}$ escaped, so $\frac{1}{4}$ were left.
      $\frac{1}{4}$ is 7 spiders, so $\frac{3}{4}$ is 21 spiders.
    b $\frac{1}{4}$ are red and $\frac{1}{2}$ are green
      so 28 are green.

CM 28

1. 6 in each half $\frac{1}{2}$ of 12 = 6
2. 4 in each quarter $\frac{1}{4}$ of 16 = 4
3. 3 in each quarter $\frac{1}{4}$ of 12 = 3
4. 7 in each quarter $\frac{1}{4}$ of 28 = 7
5. 5 in each quarter $\frac{1}{4}$ of 20 = 5
6. 9 in each half $\frac{1}{2}$ of 18 = 9

F1.3 Fractions of numbers 2

TB pages 50–51

A1   a   4   b   6
      c   5   d   10
      e   1   f   7
      g   9   h   20

A2   a   4   b   8
      c   6   d   10
      e   5   f   11
      g   7   h   1

A3   2 apples, 9 strawberries, 4 sandwiches, 6 chocolate fingers, 1 bottle of pop, 3 poppadoms

B1   Amy took 5 minutes.

B2   8 twins (4 pairs)

B3   Children's own fractions problem using $\frac{1}{3}$

C1   a   39 points
      For example:
      52 ÷ 4 = 13   13 × 3 = 39
    b   page 108
      For example:
      120 ÷ 10 = 12   120 − 12 = 108

C2   a $\frac{1}{3}$ of £39 = £13
      $\frac{1}{5}$ of £40 = £8
      I would rather have $\frac{1}{3}$ of £39
    b   Children's own 'close' fraction questions

F1.4 Fractions of quantities

TB page 52

- A1 20 cm and 5 cm
- A2 30 cm and 6 cm
- A3 50p ÷ 5 = 10p
- A4 B holds $\frac{1}{2}$ litre, C holds $\frac{1}{4}$ litre, D holds $\frac{1}{10}$ litre.
- B1 50 metres
- B2 $\frac{1}{2}$ of £1 = 50p
      $\frac{1}{10}$ of £1 = 10p
- B3 100 g
- B4 25 cm is $\frac{1}{4}$ metre
      20 cm is $\frac{1}{5}$ metre
- B5 11p
- C1 25 g butter, 65 g flour, 30 g sugar, 1 egg, $\frac{1}{2}$ teaspoon of lemon juice
- C2 a $\frac{1}{4}$ of 112 = 112 ÷ 4 = 28
        $\frac{1}{3}$ of the other number is 28, so the number is 28 × 3 = 84.
      b Children's own fraction puzzle

F1.5 Investigating fractions

TB page 53

- B1 For example:
      a $\frac{1}{4}$ of 20 = 5 and $\frac{1}{5}$ of 20 = 4
         $\frac{1}{4}$ of 100 = 25 and $\frac{1}{5}$ of 100 = 20
         $\frac{1}{4}$ is bigger than $\frac{1}{5}$.
      b $\frac{1}{5}$ of 30 = 6 and $\frac{1}{6}$ of 30 = 5
         $\frac{1}{5}$ of 60 = 12 and $\frac{1}{6}$ of 60 = 10
         $\frac{1}{5}$ is bigger than $\frac{1}{6}$.
      c $\frac{1}{7}$ of 56 = 8 and $\frac{1}{8}$ of 56 = 7
         $\frac{1}{7}$ of 560 = 80 and $\frac{1}{8}$ of 560 = 70
         $\frac{1}{7}$ is bigger than $\frac{1}{8}$.
- C1 Children will show their own examples.
      a $\frac{1}{2}$ is bigger than $\frac{2}{5}$.
      b $\frac{2}{7}$ is bigger than $\frac{1}{4}$.
- C2 Children's own 'Which would you rather have?' questions.

F2.1 Introducing decimal fractions

TB pages 54-55

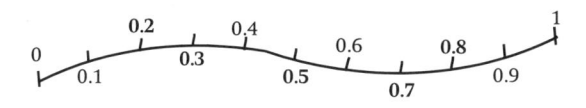

- A1 [number line from 0 to 1 marked in 0.1 intervals]
- A2 [number line from 0 to 1 with curved path through points 0.1 to 0.9]
- B1 a [vertical scale 0.3 to 1.5 in 0.1 intervals]
      b [vertical scale 0.8 to 2.1 in 0.1 intervals]
- B2 [number line from 0 to 2 marked in 0.1 intervals]
- B3 a $\frac{1}{10}$ or 0.1
      b $\frac{4}{10}$ or 0.4
      c $\frac{2}{10}$ or 0.2
      d $\frac{3}{10}$ or 0.3
- B4 a $\frac{2}{10}$ or 0.2
      b $\frac{4}{10}$ or 0.4
      c $\frac{3}{10}$ or 0.3
      d $\frac{1}{10}$ or 0.1
- C1 a Monday 0.1, Tuesday, 0.3, Wednesday 0.2, Thursday 0.4
      b none
- C2 a Jane has $\frac{1}{2}$ or $\frac{5}{10}$
         Clare has $\frac{2}{10}$
         Arash has $\frac{3}{10}$
      b Jane 0.5, Clare 0.2, Arash 0.3

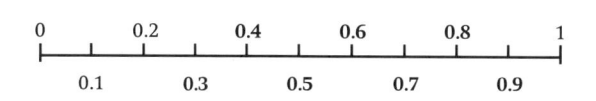

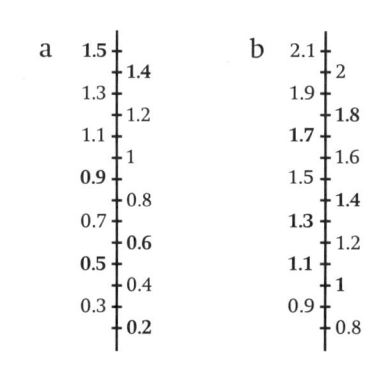

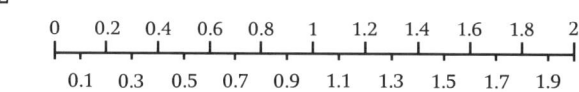

F2.2 Decimal operations
CM 30

Route through space | Name:

The rocket can zap the next asteroid in any direction by adding or subtracting to change one digit.
Find a route from Earth to Mars.

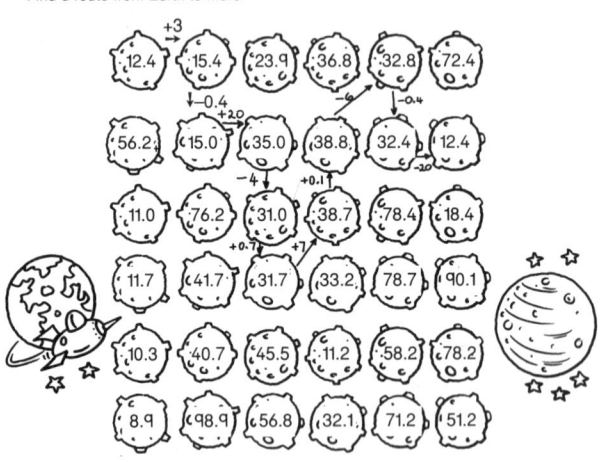

Can you find another route from a number near Earth?

Yes. 11.7 → 41.7 → 31.7 → 38.7 → 78.7 → 78.4 → 18.4

F2.4 Ordering decimals

TB page 57–58

★1 a 0.3 0.5 0.9 1.1 1.6 1.8
    b £0.15 £0.67 £1.09 £1.12 £1.45
    c 0.8 m 1.4 m 1.6 m 5.0 m 7.7 m

A1 a 0.1 0.3 0.4 0.5 0.6 0.9 1.1 1.3 1.6 1.8
    b £0.23 35p £0.59 £0.67 £1.09 £1.12 £1.45 £1.65
    c 0.8 m 1.4 m 2.5 m 3.9 m 4.1 m 5.0 m 7.7 m 8.1 m

B1 2.8 s 2.9 s 3.4 s 4.5 s 4.7 s 5.5 s 6.9 s 7.1 s 7.2 s 8.0 s

B2 £8.74 £8.64 £6.60 £6.06 £5.00 £4.61 £4.59 £3.92 £3.90 £2.99

B3 5.0 m 4.6 m 4.5 m 3.9 m 3.5 m

C1 Children's choice of prices, listed from least to most expensive

F2.5 Solving decimal problems

TB page 59

A1, A2 There are 15 possible pairs:
 a + b: 68 + 124 = 192
   length 192 cm, 1.92 m
 a + c: 68 + 245 = 313
   length 313 cm, 3.13 m
 a + d: 68 + 202 = 270
   length 270 cm, 2.70 m
 a + e: 68 + 179 = 247
   length 247 cm, 2.47 m
 a + f: 68 + 530 = 598
   length 598 cm, 5.98 m
 b + c: 124 + 245 = 369
   length 369 cm, 3.69 m
 b + d: 124 + 202 = 326
   length 326 cm, 3.26 m
 b + e: 124 + 179 = 303
   length 303 cm, 3.03 m
 b + f: 124 + 530 = 654
   length 654 cm, 6.54 m
 c + d: 245 + 202 = 447
   length 447 cm, 4.47 m
 c + e: 245 + 179 = 424
   length 424 cm, 4.24 m
 c + f: 245 + 530 = 775
   length 775 cm, 7.75 m
 d + e: 202 + 179 = 381
   length 381 cm, 3.81 m
 d + f: 202 + 530 = 732
   length 732 cm, 7.32 m
 e + f: 179 + 530 = 709
   length 709 cm, 7.09 m

B1, B2 There are 15 possible differences:
 f − a: 462 cm, 4.62 m
 f − b: 406 cm, 4.06 m
 f − c: 285 cm, 2.85 m
 f − d: 328 cm, 3.28 m
 f − e: 351 cm, 3.51 m
 c − a: 177 cm, 1.77 m
 c − b: 121 cm, 1.21 m
 c − d: 43 cm, 0.43 m
 c − e: 66 cm, 0.66 m
 d − a: 134 cm, 1.34 m
 d − b: 78 cm, 0.78 m
 d − e: 23 cm, 0.23 m
 e − a: 111 cm, 1.11 m
 e − b: 55 cm, 0.55 m
 b − a: 56 cm, 0.56 m

C1 a 272 cm, 2.72 m
    b 496 cm, 4.94 m
    c 980 cm, 9.80 m
    d 808 cm, 8.08 m
    e 716 cm, 7.16 m
    f 2120 cm, 21.20 m

C2 a 34 cm, 0.34 m
    b 62 cm, 0.62 m
    c 122.5 cm, 1.225 m
    d 101 cm, 1.01 m
    e 89.5 cm, 0.895 m
    f 265 cm, 2.65 m

F3.1 Equivalence

TB pages 60–61

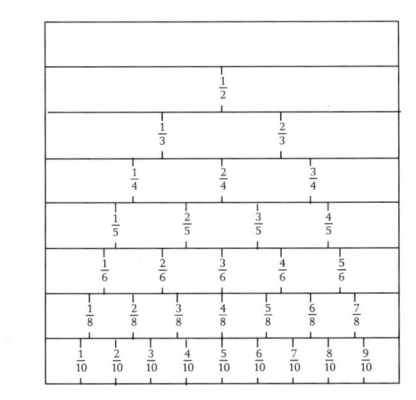

A1 [fraction wall diagram showing halves, thirds, quarters, fifths, sixths, eighths and tenths]

A2 a $\frac{1}{2}$ is the same as $\frac{2}{4}, \frac{3}{6}, \frac{4}{8}$ and $\frac{5}{10}$
    b $\frac{1}{3}$ is the same as $\frac{2}{6}$
    c $\frac{1}{5}$ is the same as $\frac{2}{10}$

A3 $\frac{2}{8}$ is the same as $\frac{1}{4}$
    $\frac{6}{8}$ is the same as $\frac{3}{4}$
    $\frac{2}{3}$ is the same as $\frac{4}{6}$
    $\frac{3}{5}$ is the same as $\frac{6}{10}$

B1 a $\frac{2}{4}$ or $\frac{1}{2}$
    b $\frac{2}{6}$ or $\frac{1}{3}$
    c $\frac{4}{6}$ or $\frac{2}{3}$
    d $\frac{6}{10}$ or $\frac{3}{5}$
    e $\frac{6}{8}$ or $\frac{3}{4}$

C1 $\frac{3}{4}, \frac{5}{8}, \frac{2}{3}$ and $\frac{5}{6}$ are greater than $\frac{1}{2}$

C2 b $\frac{3}{12}$ is the same as $\frac{2}{8}$ and $\frac{1}{4}$
       $\frac{4}{12}$ is the same as $\frac{2}{6}$ and $\frac{1}{3}$
       $\frac{9}{12}$ is the same as $\frac{3}{4}$ and $\frac{6}{8}$
       $\frac{6}{15}$ is the same as $\frac{4}{10}$ and $\frac{2}{5}$
       $\frac{12}{15}$ is the same as $\frac{8}{10}$ and $\frac{4}{5}$

F3.2 Ordering familiar fractions

TB page 62

A1 e holds the least.

A2 c holds the most.

A3 b, e and f hold less than $\frac{1}{2}$ l.

B1 a Georgina is oldest.
    b Charlie is youngest.
    c Hari is older than Fred.
    d Baskar is younger than Eliza.
    e Baskar, Jane, Eliza
    f Dexter and Georgina
    g Fred

B2 a Elspeth finished first.
    b Annie took longest.
    c Ben was quicker than Carrie.
    d No, Dan finished before Carrie.

CM 35

1 [number line: $3\frac{1}{4}$ $3\frac{2}{4}$ $3\frac{3}{4}$ 4 $4\frac{1}{4}$ $4\frac{2}{4}$ $4\frac{3}{4}$ 5 $5\frac{1}{4}$ $5\frac{2}{4}$ $5\frac{3}{4}$ 6]

   [number line: $1\frac{1}{5}$ $1\frac{2}{5}$ $1\frac{3}{5}$ $1\frac{4}{5}$ 2 $2\frac{1}{5}$ $2\frac{2}{5}$ $2\frac{3}{5}$ $2\frac{4}{5}$ 3 $3\frac{1}{5}$ $3\frac{2}{5}$]

   [number line: 2 $2\frac{1}{3}$ $2\frac{2}{3}$ 3 $3\frac{1}{3}$ $3\frac{2}{3}$ 4 $4\frac{1}{3}$ $4\frac{2}{3}$ 5 $5\frac{1}{3}$ $5\frac{2}{3}$]

   [number line: $\frac{7}{10}$ $\frac{8}{10}$ $\frac{9}{10}$ 1 $1\frac{1}{10}$ $1\frac{2}{10}$ $1\frac{3}{10}$ $1\frac{4}{10}$ $1\frac{5}{10}$ $1\frac{6}{10}$ $1\frac{7}{10}$ $1\frac{8}{10}$]

   [number line: $1\frac{7}{8}$ 2 $2\frac{1}{8}$ $2\frac{2}{8}$ $2\frac{3}{8}$ $2\frac{4}{8}$ $2\frac{5}{8}$ $2\frac{6}{8}$ $2\frac{7}{8}$ 3 $3\frac{1}{8}$ $3\frac{2}{8}$]

2 For example:
   $\frac{8}{10} = \frac{4}{5}$ $1\frac{2}{10} = 1\frac{1}{5}$
   $1\frac{4}{10} = 1\frac{2}{5}$ $1\frac{5}{10} = 1\frac{1}{2}$
   $1\frac{6}{10} = 1\frac{3}{5}$ $1\frac{8}{10} = 1\frac{4}{5}$
   $2\frac{2}{8} = 2\frac{1}{4}$ $2\frac{4}{8} = 2\frac{1}{2}$
   $2\frac{6}{8} = 2\frac{3}{4}$ $3\frac{2}{8} = 3\frac{1}{4}$

F3.4 Introducing proportion

TB page 63

A1 a In every week I spend **5** days at school.
   b In every 2 weeks I spend **10** days at school.
   c In every 3 weeks I spend **15** days at school.

A2 a 6 lemon sweets
   b 12 lemon sweets
   c 30 lemon sweets

B1 a For every 4 laps they have walked 2 miles.
   b For every 8 laps they have walked 4 miles.
   c For every 6 laps they have walked 3 miles.
   d For every 10 laps they have walked 5 miles.

CM 37

1. The shorter track is $\frac{1}{2}$ of the longer track. The longer track is 2 times the shorter track.
2. The shorter track is $\frac{1}{10}$ of the longer track. The longer track is 10 times the shorter track.
3. The shorter track is $\frac{1}{3}$ of the longer track. The longer track is 3 times the shorter track.
4. The shorter track is $\frac{1}{4}$ of the longer track. The longer track is 4 times the shorter track.
5. The shorter track is $\frac{2}{3}$ of the longer track. The longer track is $1\frac{1}{2}$ times the shorter track.

F3.5 Using proportion to solve problems

TB page 64

A1 a You need 2 cups of rice for 8 people.
   b You need $\frac{1}{2}$ cup of rice for 2 people.

A2 a You need 9 cups of water for 3 cups of rice.
   b You need $1\frac{1}{2}$ cups of water for $\frac{1}{2}$ cup of rice.

A3 a She used 2 cups of rice.
   b She was cooking for 8 people.

B1 a He will give her £4 when she has saved £20.
   b She must have saved £50 before he gives her £10.
   c He will give her £7 when she has saved £35.
   d She will have £120 with the money from her grandfather.

C1 Children's altered recipes

CM 38

For 36 cakes you need:
300 g butter or margerine
150 g soft brown sugar
300 g honey
grated rind and juice of 3 lemons
6 eggs
675 g self-raising flour
3 teaspoons baking powder